THE WATER FACTORY

Written by:

John R. Sheaffer, PhD

Illustrated by:

Ronald C. Sheaffer

This book is dedicated to
Verna and Cheryl.

Thank you!

The boy who wonders
and his sidekick Lucy.

I wonder where they make all this new water? Do you think there is a water factory somewhere?
Lucy, let's go find out!

Road trip!

Look!
There it is, the water factory!
This must be where they make
new water!

5

They usually charge more
for the water than the gasoline!

Well that was interesting, but we still don't know where they make new water.
Okay Lucy, find the water factory!

7

We don't make water; we **<u>GET WATER!!</u>**
People **<u>NEED</u>** water; they can't live without it.
So we **<u>GET</u>** it for them!!

We have dug wells hundreds of feet deep, changed the flow of entire rivers, built dams, and laid thousands of miles of pipe to move water! We drained lakes, made lakes, and we will do it again and again, because **WE HAVE TO HAVE WATER!!**

We have spent billions of dollars to do it and we will spend billions more to keep doing it. We pipe water into every house, restaurant, playground, factory, school, store and business , because...

PEOPLE NEED WATER!!

It is an engineering marvel!!!

Now think about what we use water for besides drinking and cooking. We wash our dirty hands and bodies with it. We brush our teeth in it, clean our dirty clothes, dishes, pots, pans and floors with it, and we go potty in it!!

So, after everybody uses the water, we bring it all back; we separate it ,filter it, churn it, stir it, shake it, grind it, and spin it!!

My, oh my, the money it costs, the energy we use, everyday, week, month, and year!!

It is truly amazing!

We dump it into an
ocean or a river.
We throw it all out!!

What do you do with the
water after all that effort
and money?

13

I'm so confused, it all seems so wasteful. What will we do if we run out of water _and_ money?

We _have_ to find a water factory.

I know! Let's go ask the professor. He should know if there's a water factory!

Well it sounds like you two have had a most interesting adventure.

Come along with me, and I'll take you to the "water factory."

WHOO HOO!!!

We're going to the water factory!!!

Let me explain. All water is used water. Water flows from the rivers into the oceans, where it evaporates, forms clouds and makes rain. The rain falls to the earth and runs off the land into the rivers and returns to the oceans completing the cycle.

The thing you have to understand is that all the water that ever was, or ever will be, has been here since the earth was formed.

We can't "make" water.

All water is used water. You probably never had a glass that did not go through seven Native Americans, twelve settlers and fifty buffalo before you got it.

It looks like I will have
to do some more explaining.

People need water to live, and the crops that we depend on for our food need water to grow. So, we have to manage the available water so that both of these needs are met.

Since we use water to carry away our potty, it is full of bacteria, germs and nutrients. Now you do not want that dirty water to stay in your house, so we collect all the used water and bring it back to a "sanitary district". The districts treat it for a short time, killing the bacteria and germs, and then dump the still nutrient rich water into our creeks, rivers and oceans, where it causes water pollution.

If we need nutrients to grow food, why are we using them to hurt fish?

Since there is no "new water,"
we must manage our available water.

How are we going to do that?

25

Before you panic, what if we stopped throwing all that used water away. What if we just borrowed it, then gave it to the farmers with nutrients for their plants already in it. All we have to do is change the final treatment step from our rivers to our farms!

We need to recycle the nutrients that are in our wastewater to grow crops. When they are in our water systems they are pollutants. On our land they are resources.

POWER PLANT

STORAGE LAGOON

AERATION

AERATION

RIVER

SPRAY IRRIGATION

CROPS

We would have millions of gallons of nutrient-rich water for growing crops. We can stop polluting our rivers and streams. We will not be as dependent on the weather and the very ground you are standing on will grow crops, recycle nutrients, and take carbon dioxide out of the air, reducing air pollution. Do you realize that how we manage our wastewater affects the cost of growing our food?

So you see there really is a water factory! It not only reclaims and cleans our wastewater, it conserves energy by recycling nutrients, and it cleans the air by taking out carbon dioxide and helps reduce global warming!

Then farmers and cities will not have to fight over water. After the people in the cities use the water the farmers can reclaim and reuse the nitrogen and phosphorus, the very things plants need to grow!

It is up to you! Let's get moving to make it happen!

It is the national goal that the discharge of pollutants into navigable waters be eliminated!

Dr. John R. "Jack" Sheaffer received his Ph.D. from the University of Chicago, Chicago, Illinois. He was instrumental in the formulation of the landmark Clean Water Act Amendments and served as the Scientific Advisor to the Secretary of the Army and was decorated for Exceptional Civilian Service. He was awarded an honorary Doctor Honoris Causa from The Academic Council of the University of Forestry, Sofia Bulgaria and is a member of the Cosmos Club in Washington D.C.

He is the author or co-author of ten books and more than sixty technical papers on wastewater management, irrigation, flood proofing and comprehensive water resources management. He currently lives in Wheaton, Illinois with his wife Verna.

Ronald C. Sheaffer received his BA. from Wheaton College, Wheaton, Illinois. He served as a U.S. Army Infantry Captain, Airborne and was an All Army Art Award winner. He founded a lake restoration business and was awarded a U.S. Patent. His wife Cheryl still lets him live with her in Sandwich, Illinois and he does not know why.